Talking About
Racism

Nicola Edwards

Chrysalis Children's Books

First published in the UK in 2003 by

(●) Chrysalis Children's Books

The Chrysalis Building, Bramley Road, London W10 6SP

Copyright © Chrysalis Books PLC 2003

ISBN 184138 8254

British Library Cataloguing in Publication Data for this book is available from the British Library.

A BELITHA BOOK

Editorial manager: Joyce Bentley
Senior editor: Sarah Nunn
Picture researchers: Terry Forshaw, Lois Charlton
Designer: Wladek Szechter
Editor: Kate Phelps
Consultant: Dr Ute Navidi, Head of Policy, ChildLine

Printed in China

The pictures used in this book do not show the actual people named in the text.

Foreword

People are not born racists. Racist behaviour is learned; racist attitudes are based on ignorance and fear of others. Through vivid, topical examples **Talking About Racism** shows that racism hurts people. Children can hurt each other by name-calling as well as physical attacks. Making fun of or bullying other children because they look, speak or behave differently is also unfair.

Talking About Racism enables adults, teachers and children to talk about racism and inequality and helps tackle racist attitudes before they become entrenched. It reinforces schools' anti-bullying strategies by emphasising respect and friendship. Speaking out about racism takes courage, and by identifying someone they can talk to safely – a trusted adult, a friend of their own age or ChildLine – children take the first step towards finding help for themselves or their friends.

But **Talking About Racism** goes beyond confronting racist bullying at school. Highlighting the feelings of refugee and asylum-seeking children exemplifies the global context. And, from racist abuse shouted at football matches to anti-racist demonstrations, this book reflects wider social attitudes.

Informative and thought-provoking, the **Talking About** series tackles some disturbing aspects of contemporary society: racism, domestic violence, divorce, eating problems and bullying. Adults often try to protect children from these problems or believe they will not understand. Taking children through a series of situations they can identify with – using words and images – also means offering alternative ways of resolving conflict. Each book shows that even very young children are not passive observers or victims but want to make sense of their world and act to make life better for themselves, their families and other children.

Ute Navidi, Head of Policy, ChildLine

Contents

What is racism?

Racism is treating someone differently or unfairly because of the colour of their skin or the country they come from. Racism often leads to **bullying**.

These children shouted insults at Jade because she is black.

When Louis was new at school, children bullied him because he is French.

Racist bullies pick on people and call them names. They may attack people by punching or kicking them or throwing things at them.

Making fun

Children often pick on others they see as being different in some way. They may wear different clothes or eat different foods because of their family background or religion.

Yasmin was proud to be a **Muslim**. But she didn't like it when some people stared at her and her family in the street.

Children made fun of Ali. They didn't like the food he brought to school.

Children sometimes laugh at things they find strange or unusual. But what seems like harmless fun to one person can make someone else very upset.

It's no joke

Sometimes, when bullies are told off about their behaviour, they say that they were just messing around. They try to make people think that they didn't mean any harm.

Robert thought it was funny to laugh at his friend Conor's Irish accent.

James was treated unfairly by children who knew nothing about him except what he looked like.

They say the person they were bullying can't take a joke. But racist bullying makes people feel sad, **lonely** and frightened.

Bullying is always wrong. Don't be a bully.

Not just in school

Racism is a big problem in the world today. It causes pain and suffering to many people. Racists think that they are more important than others who come from a different **culture**.

IN MEMORY OF
STEPHEN LAWRENCE
13.9.1974
22.4.1993
MAY HE REST IN PEACE

Stephen Lawrence was a young black man who was killed in the street by a **gang** of racists.

Racists hate these other people and think they have the right to attack them.

This girl from a **refugee** family had to leave her home and come to a country where she did not feel welcome.

Why are people racist?

People are not born racists. Racism is an attitude that develops in some people as they grow up. It is often learnt from family or friends.

These marchers are complaining about people from other countries coming to live in Britain.

Racists set fire to this shop owned
by an Asian family.

Racists are ignorant of other cultures
and often frightened by what they
do not understand.

Safe at home?

Everyone has the right to feel safe.
But sometimes racists try to upset and frighten
people in their homes by smashing their
windows or spraying nasty messages on walls.

Sometimes racists
can make people feel very worried and
afraid even in their own homes.

Racists sometimes attack buildings where people **worship** too.

שויתי ה" לנגדי תמיד

This **synagogue** is a holy building for Jewish people. It was attacked by racists.

Racist attacks are against the **law**. Police officers will try to catch the racists.

Racism in the street

People often have to cope with racism while they are trying to get on with their everyday lives.

Ross was worried about being bullied by racists on the way home from school. His friend, Sean, said they could travel back together, in a group of friends.

Some footballers say they experience racist **abuse** at football matches.

Racists are **cowards**. They need to feel part of a group. Racist gangs may throw things at people in the street, punch them or damage their cars, simply because they look or speak differently.

How does it feel?

Racist bullying can make children feel sad and lonely. They may feel that they can't tell anyone at home about it because they don't want to worry or upset them. Children may even feel angry with their parents for giving them their skin colour.

Racist bullies made Imrie feel sad and angry.

Bullies made Lisa feel
ashamed that her dad is black.

Being bullied can make people
feel **ashamed** and worthless.

Sometimes people that are bullied may pretend to
be ill, refuse to go to school or refuse to go out to
play because of the bullying.

Don't stand for it

Racism is wrong and no one should have to put up with it. Racist bullies like people to see them bullying someone. It makes them feel important.

These people are marching to show that they are against racism.

If you are being bullied,
it is brave to tell someone. It is not
telling tales.

People can help to stop bullies by refusing
to stand by and watch it happen.

If you are bullied, or if you
see bullying in school, tell
an adult you **trust**.

Beating racism

Teachers know that racist bullying can happen in schools. They must help children who are bullied. Headteachers can let everyone in the school know that racism is wrong and that it is not allowed.

The head teacher told the children that they are all equal and that everyone has a part to play in stamping out racist bullying in school.

Bullies are less likely to pick on people who look **confident** and **determined**.

Children can help stop racist bullying by showing **respect** to others and ignoring racists.

If someone tries to bully you, shout 'GO AWAY!', and then tell a teacher.

Learning from each other

Racism sometimes happens because people do not understand or respect how other people live or what they believe.

These children enjoyed finding out how **Hindu** people celebrate **Diwali**.

Balraj invited his friend, Caitlin, to his sister's wedding.

People are happier when they offer each other friendship and respect.

The world is a richer place exactly because it is made up of billions of different people, each with their own history and background and personality.

Teamwork

Everyone is different, with their own special strengths and **talents**. It makes people happy when others show them respect by being polite and friendly.

Great things can happen when people respect each other's differences and value each other's talents.

These football players work as a team and show respect for each other.

Think about what makes you special and what you like about your friends.

Everyone has the right to live without fear. People can work together to fight against racism.

Good friends

Some children get very upset when their friends are bullied by racists. Children who have been bullied say their friends helped them to cope and change things for the better.

Children can work together
to build a future without racism.

The world is a happier place when people of all races can love one another and live together without fear.

It's important for everyone to feel that they have friends who care about them and respect them.

Words to remember

abuse Words or actions that harm someone.

ashamed Feeling bad, as if you have done something wrong.

bullying Hurting someone or making them feel sad.

confident Feeling as if you can do anything.

coward Someone who acts as if they are brave when they are in a crowd but who is easily afraid when on their own.

culture The ideas, skills, arts and way of life of certain groups of people.

determined Strongly intending to do something.

Diwali An important festival in the Hindu religion.

gang A group of people.

Hindu A follower of Hinduism, one of the world's major religions.

law The rules of a country.

lonely Feeling sad, as if you have no friends.

Muslim A follower of the religion of Islam.

refugees People who have left their own country because it is not safe.

respect To think well of people and be polite to them.

synagogue A building where Jewish people worship.

talents The things that a person is good at.

trust Feeling that someone won't let you down.

worship Praying and giving thanks to God.

Organisations, helplines and websites

FOR CHILDREN:
ChildLine
A charity offering information, help and advice to any child with worries or problems.
Address for adults:
45 Folgate Street, London E1 6GL
Address for children:
Freepost NATN1111, London E1 6BR
Free and confidential helpline for children and young people: 0800 1111
ChildLine Scotland bullying helpline:
0800 441111
www.childline.org.uk

Anne Frank Educational Trust
Promotes anti-racism education and positive attitudes towards difference.
PO Box 11880, London N6 4LN
www.afet.org.uk

Britkid
Website covering a range of race and racism issues aimed at young people and teachers.
www.britkid.org

Bullying Online
Offers support and advice to children, parents, teachers and youth leaders. Help for bullies and their parents too.
www.bullying.co.uk

FOR PARENTS:
ChildLine
45 Folgate Street, London E1 6GL

Black Information Link
Website run by the 1990 Trust covering human rights and anti-racism issues.
www.blink.org.uk

Campaign Against Racism and Fascism
Anti-racist on-line magazine with resources and information.
www.carf.demon.co.uk

Commission for Racial Equality
Non-governmental organisation tackling racial discrimination, promoting equality and advising on race issues.
St Dunstan's House
201–211 Borough High Street
London SE1 1GZ
www.cre.gov.uk

Crosspoint Anti Racism
Website dealing with human rights and anti-racism issues, with links to over 2000 organisations in 113 countries.
www.magenta.nl/crosspoint

Institute of Race Relations
Publishes on-line resources.
www.irr.org.uk

Parentline Plus
Offers help, support and information to anyone parenting a child.
Helpline: 0808 800 2222
www.parentlineplus.org.uk

The Runnymede Trust
Independent think tank on ethnicity.
Suite 106
The London Fruit and Wool Exchange
Brushfield Street
London E1 6EP
www.runnymedetrust.org

Index

Picture credits
Front cover (main) David Hoffman, front cover left to right: Bubbles/Angela Hampton, Bubbles/Pauline Cutler (two), John Birdsall, 4 Bubbles/Pauline Cutler, 5 Corbis/William Gottlieb, 6 Corbis/Peter Turnley, 7 John Birdsall, 8 Corbis/Rick Gomez, 9 Bubbles/Angela Hampton, 10 Photofusion/Sam Appleby, 11 Corbis/David Turnley, 12-15 David Hoffman, 16 Corbis/Richard Hutchings, 17 Empics, 18 Bubbles/Pauline Cutler, 19 John Birdsall, 20 Photofusion/Bob Watkins, 21 Bubbles/Pauline Cutler, 22 John Birdsall, 23 Format/Jacky Chapman, 24 Photofusion/Brian Mitchell, 25 Corbis/Richard Olivier, 26 John Birdsall, 27 Rex Features/Mark Pain, 28 Bubbles